Badger Key Stage 3 Geography Starters

Book Two

Fred Martin, Lisa Mitchell, Charlotte Togni and Gary Dawson

Badger Publishing Limited
26 Wedgwood Way, Pin Green Industrial Estate, Stevenage, Hertfordshire SG1 4QF
Telephone: 01438 356907 Fax: 01438 747015.

Cover photograph: Twelve Apostles, Australia © G. Hellier,
Robert Harding Picture Library.

Introduction

The Badger *Geography Starters* aim to provide teachers with a bank of practical ideas that can be used as starter activities during KS3, either as they are written, or adapted. The geographical content of the books is based on the KS3 Programme of Study in the National Curriculum Orders for Geography. The choice of topics comes from both the Breadth of Study section in the Programme of Study and from the QCA Schemes of Work.

The choice of topics for each book reflects a likely sequence that could be taught in each year. They can, however, be used in a more flexible way, for example, by using activities from several books with any one year group. Where this is done, teachers may need to modify the level of difficulty of the activities.

The idea of using starters is an integral part of the Foundation Subjects strand of the KS3 Strategy. The starter activity is intended to engage and develop an initial interest in a topic. Each starter activity should last between 5-10 minutes. However, although the book only focuses on the starter, the lesson needs to be seen as a whole to include its main activities and a plenary. The activity sheets contain some suggestions as to how the lesson can develop, as well as ideas that aim to challenge some students.

Three key principles lie behind the kind of content and activities that are effective as starters:

- They should build on and link to what the students already know. This can be from previous work in Geography or in other subjects. It can also be from the students' own personal experiences, for example in the local area.

- They should aim to capture interest quickly. This can be done, for example, by using strong, visually stimulating resources, or by subject matter that although unusual, may serve to introduce and illustrate a wider point.

- They should engage the students by involving them in activities that require them to think, including asking their own questions.

Some of the activities are relatively simple and require little preparation, for example showing a photograph or map from the Copymaster resource. Others involve the preparation of cards and other resources. The latter can be laminated for future use.

The use of a data projector and interactive whiteboard is recommended for some activities. These are resources that have enormous potential in the Geography classroom. If they are not available, teachers will need to find an alternative technique, but present a justification for getting them.

As well as having educational value, starter activities can be fun for both the teacher and the student. So aim to enjoy them!

Fred Martin

Main Theme	Unit	NC PoS	Theme content	Graphic skills NC PoS 2	QCA SoW	Student activities	Scale	KS3 Strategy strands	Thinking Skills
Shaping the land	1.1	1a, 6c	geographical questions		8	using images to ask geographical questions	R,G	L	P, C
	1.2	1a, 6c	coastal conundrum		8	solving a puzzle	L	L	C, R, E
	1.3	6c	key word 'jeopardy'		8	using key geographical vocabulary	G	L	P, R, E
	1.4	6c	transportation and deposition		8	description of geographical features	G	L	P, R, C, E
	1.5	1a, 6c	a risky business		8	asking geographical questions	R	L	P, R, C
	1.6	1a, 6c	Read all about it!		8	brainstorm coastal management techniques	N	L	R, E, P, C
Tectonic hazards	2.1	6c	structure	diagram	2	define words, key terms	G	L	P
	2.2	6b	activity		2	define words, link ideas, apply concepts	G	L, ICT	C, P, R
	2.3	6b	impacts	atlas, map, data	2	analyse data, analyse map, sort information	I	L, C	E, P
	2.4	6b	impacts	photo	2	analyse photo, responses	G	L, C	P, R, C, E
	2.5	6b	management		2	card sorting, rank, explain	G	C	P, R, E
	2.6	6b	benefits	atlas	2	sort information, analyse	G	C	P, R, E
Measuring wealth	3.1	1a, 6i	quality of life		12,16	ranking information	G	L	P, R, E
	3.2	1d, 6i	money, money, money		12,16	ranking information	G	L	R, E
	3.3	1a, 2d, 6i	challenging stereotypes		12,16	classifying images, reasoning and evaluation	G	L	C, R
	3.4	1d, 6i	development dominoes		12,16	reasoning, matching countries to statistics	G	N	C, R, P, E
	3.5	2d, 6i	stepping into a photograph		12,16	asking geographical questions, developing a sense of empathy	G	L	C
	3.6	6i	Fact? Fiction? Opinion?		12,16	reasoning, evaluation, processing	G	L	P, R, E
The green planet	4.1	6e	savanna ecosystem	diagram	14	define, describe, explain, analyse, link ideas, discuss	I	L	P, R
	4.2	6e	soil		14	analyse, link ideas		L	P, R, C
	4.3	6e	world's ecosystems	map	14	describe, analyse, draw, compare	G		P, R, E
	4.4	6d, 6e	climate and ecosystems	graph	14	describe, interpret, explain, analyse, sort, discuss	I	L	P, R
	4.5	6e	human impacts on ecosystems		14	explain, sort, compare, discuss	G	L	P, R
	4.6	6e	coral reef ecosystems	diagram	14	define, describe, explain, interpret, discuss	G	L	P, R, C
The world's citizens	5.1	6fi	perceptions		3	sorting fact and opinion	G	L	R
	5.2	6fii	increase	data table	3	calculations	G	N	P
	5.3	6f1	world totals	graphs	3	reading a graph	G	N	P
	5.4	6fiii	resources		3, 14	understanding issues	G	N	E
	5.5	6f1	density	data table	3	calculations using ICT	G	N, ICT	P
	5.6	6fii	movement	photo	3	photo interpretation	G	L	C

Notes

NC PoS: themes selected from the Breadth of Study section of the NC PoS.

QCA SoA: main focus for the unit in relation to the optional QCA KS3 SoW.

Scale: Local-L, Regional-R, National-N, International-I, Global-G.

KS3 Strategy strands: where there is a particular focus on one of these strands: Literacy (L), Numeracy (N), ICT (ICT).

Thinking skills: selected references to Processing P, Reasoning R, Creative C, Evaluation E.

Contents

Shaping the land

Tectonic hazards

Measuring wealth

The green planet

The world's citizens

Asking geographical questions

Objective:

To introduce some basic coastal features and to raise questions about the processes that shape them.

Teaching point:

The activity aims to help the students to develop an enquiry approach to learning by providing a simple framework to use for asking geographical questions.

What you will need:
OHT of Copymaster 1.1.

Time:
5 minutes

Key words: what, where, when, why, who, how

Activity:

a) Display an OHT of Copymaster 1.1 showing a coastal landscape. This particular image is the Twelve Apostles in Australia, but don't tell students this fact yet as it may form one of their questions.

b) Students are to write 6 questions about the photo. They should use the 5Ws and an H approach to help them, i.e. their questions should begin as follows:

- What?
- Where?
- When?
- Why?
- Who?
- How?

c) For feedback, the students should share some of their questions with the rest of the class. Their questions could be written on the board surrounding the image.

Challenge: The students should try to answer the questions their neighbour has written.

Take it forward: This starter provides a useful introduction to a unit of work on coasts. The students should be reminded to use the '5Ws and an H' approach throughout the unit.

© Robert Harding Picture Library

A coastal conundrum

Objective:

To understand that coastlines change and to learn about the processes that form caves, arches, stacks and stumps.

What you will need:
OHT of Copymaster 1.2.

Time:
5 minutes

Teaching point:

Coastlines are dynamic features that are constantly being changed by weathering and erosion. The students may find that the time scale for change, although rapid in geological terms, can be hard to detect within their more limited experiences of time. Nevertheless, evidence of change can often be apparent.

Key words: weathering, erosion, fault, cave, arch, stack, stump, headland, bay, hydraulic action, corrasion, abrasion, corrosion

Activity:

a) Show the students an OHT of Copymaster 1.2. Tell them that this is a puzzle for them to solve. Ask the question, 'How did the man get there?' Tell them that he cannot swim, he didn't use any vehicle (boat, plane, helicopter etc), he didn't use ropes and it's too far to jump, so how did he get there?

b) The students are to find an answer to the puzzle. Encourage them to share their suggestions. Some classes may need steering towards the idea of natural processes. This will largely depend on their prior learning. Expect the bizarre, e.g. alien abduction, as well as more plausible responses.

c) After a reasonable number of suggestions, point out how old the man is (over 100), and inform the students that the stack used to be part of the mainland. The puzzle should be used as an introduction to thinking about erosional processes. It should be made clear to the students that this process doesn't happen over night!

Challenge: The students could put a series of coastal images in chronological order, i.e. from headland to cave, arch, stack and stump.

Take it forward: Use this starter as a quick, 'fun' introduction to a lesson on the formation of coastal landforms.

Key word 'jeopardy'

Objective:

To revise the key terms associated with coastal geomorphology.

Teaching point:

Techniques adapted from game shows are often a good way to develop an interest in a tropic. This activity uses the US game show 'Jeopardy' as its starting point. The students should be able to draw on previous knowledge to give definitions of key terms associated with coastal geomorphology.

What you will need:
Copymaster 1.3. The key terms need to be cut up either as an OHT or as sets of cards.

Time:
5-10 minutes

Key words: hydraulic action, abrasion, corrasion, corrosion, stack, stump, arch, headland, bay, longshore drift, swash, backwash, beach, cave, wave-cut notch, wave-cut platform, fetch, spit, erosion, deposition, transportation

Activity:

a) Divide the students into pairs or groups and give them a set of the word cards. An alternative approach is to use the cards as a whole class activity.

b) The students should write questions that could be asked to go with each of the words on the cards. Example:

   Answer: Longshore drift

   Question: What is the name of the process that transports sediment along a coastline?

c) Review their questions to see which would be the most effective. Different criteria for 'effectiveness' could be created, e.g. the shortest, the strangest, the most obvious, the most humorous, etc.

Challenge: The students could add more key terms and pass them on to a partner to write the questions. Students could also group similar terms together, e.g. features formed by processes of erosion, transport and deposition.

Take it forward: To consolidate their knowledge and understanding of the key terms, at the end of the lesson, the students could work in different pairs/groups and use their questions to test other students.

Erosion	Headland
Transportation	Bay
Deposition	Wave-cut platform
Hydraulic action	Wave-cut notch
Corrasion/abrasion	Weathering
Corrosion	Spit
Stack	Arch
Longshore drift	Beach
Stump	Fetch
Cave	Swash

Transportation and deposition

Objective:

To understand that processes of transportation and deposition create distinctive landforms.

Teaching point:

This lesson needs to be linked to one that explains how a coastline is eroded and how longshore drift moves the eroded material along the coast.

What you will need:
An OHT of Copymaster 1.4.

Time:
5 minutes

Key words: spit, transportation, deposition, longshore drift, swash, backwash, sediment

Activity:

a) Show the students an OHT of Copymaster 1.4. This shows a photo of the Varadero Beach, in the Matanzas Province, Cuba.

b) The students are to list adjectives that could be used to describe the spit. Encourage them to consider colour, shape, texture, direction etc. The students could add their adjectives to the board, or each student could be provided with a worksheet that shows the image.

c) As feedback, the students share their word bank with the rest of the class, gradually building up a list of adjectives on the board. The students then choose the 5 adjectives they think best describe the spit.

Challenge: The students write a paragraph to describe and suggest how the spit was formed, using the word bank created at the start of the lesson. They could find Varadero Beach on an atlas map to get further details of its shape, size and the materials it could be made from.

Take it forward: The starter could be used to introduce a lesson on longshore drift and the formation of spits. Atlas maps, satellite images and other maps could be used to compare the features of spits in different locations.

Transportation and deposition

© Donald Nausbaum / Getty Images

A risky business

Objective:

To understand how coastal erosion can impact upon the human environment.

What you will need:
An OHT of Copymaster 1.5.

Time:
10 minutes

Teaching point:

This activity aims to provide a starting point for generating discussion as to how coastal processes can impact upon the human environment, notably the economy and society.

Key words: boulder clay, erosion, glacial till, deposition, Ice Age, economy, insurance, society, agriculture

Activity:

a) Inform the students that the Holderness Coastline is one of the world's fastest eroding coastlines. One of the reasons for the rapid rate of erosion is that the cliffs are made from boulder clay, an unconsolidated glacial till deposited at the end of the last Ice Age.

b) Display the image of Mrs Sue Earle standing by the remains of her farm at Mappleton. Students are to take the role of investigative journalists from a national newspaper, and list the questions they would like to ask Mrs Earle. (It might be useful here to remind students of the '5Ws and an H' questioning they used in starter 1.1.)

Challenge: The teacher, or a student, could take the 'hot seat' and play Mrs Earle whilst other students ask their questions.

Take it forward: This starter could form the introduction to a more detailed study of the Holderness Coast. In particular, the study could raise questions about the methods, costs and value of attempts to control the rate of erosion. The issue could be considered from a variety of perspectives and at different scales, e.g. local and national.

A risky business

© Press Association Photos

Read all about it!

Objective:

To investigate the merits of different coastal management techniques.

Teaching point:

This activity assumes that students already have some knowledge of coastal management techniques. It should be used to draw together some of the issues surrounding coastal management.

What you will need:
An OHT of Copymaster 1.6.

Time:
5 minutes

Key words: managed retreat, coastal management, sea wall, groyne, revetment

Activity:

a) Display OHT 1.6, a series of headlines relating to coastal management in one location (Bournemouth).

b) The students are to try to guess what the story is about, using each of the headlines as evidence for what has happened. They could write their answers down, or this exercise can be done as a quick whole class brainstorm.

Challenge: The students could take one of the headlines and continue the rest of the story.

Take it forward: Discuss the advantages and disadvantages of different types of coastal management techniques, perhaps with a decision-making exercise.

ROW BREAKS OUT OVER COASTAL DEFENCES
Wednesday, 12 March, 2003, 11:09 GMT

From: www.news.bbc.co.uk

Tide holes town's sea wall
Saturday, 12 October, 2002, 08:35 GMT

From: http://news.bbc.co.uk/1/hi/england/2321363.stm

Letting the sea protect the land
Friday, 11 October, 2002

From: http://news.bbc.co.uk/1/hi/sci/tech/2317397.stm

Price to pay for living on the edge
26 January, 2003

From: http://observer.guardian.co.uk/cash/story/0,6903,882199,00.html

Barrier reef proposed for Bournemouth
15 June, 2000

From: http://news.bbc.co.uk/1/hi/uk/792095.stm

The Earth's interior

Objective:

To know the key words used to describe the structure of the Earth.

What you will need:
Copies of Copymaster 2.1.

Time:
5 minutes

Teaching point:

This activity aims to reinforce prior learning and emphasise key vocabulary.

Key words: plate, mantle, volcano, crust, fault, core, earthquake, fold mountains, trench, ridge

Activity:

a) Hand out a copy of Copymaster 2.1 to each student. Remind them of contexts in which they have previously studied this topic.

b) The students fill in answers on the sheet using the jumbled words in the Jumbled Word-bank. Alternatively this activity can be conducted as a class with an enlarged or OHT copy of the Copymaster.

c) Consider the questions that can be asked about each of the features, for example, how uniform they are in thickness, what the materials consist of, how quickly they move, etc.

Unjumbled word bank!

epatl = plate	lemnat = mantle
calvono = volcano	sctru = crust
auflt = fault	eroc = core
reqarutkaeh = earthquake	mlou fdotninas = fold mountains
thrnce = trench	idrge = ridge
ceaonic = oceanic	oncintalten = continental
nneri = inner	terou = outer
ilacsd ran = island arc	frnf eg ioir = ring of fire

Challenge: Write a set of crossword clues to go with each of the key words.

Take it forward: Develop the lesson by studying the processes that create each of the features. This will help to develop an understanding of earthquakes and volcanoes, their effects and the extent to which their effects can be managed.

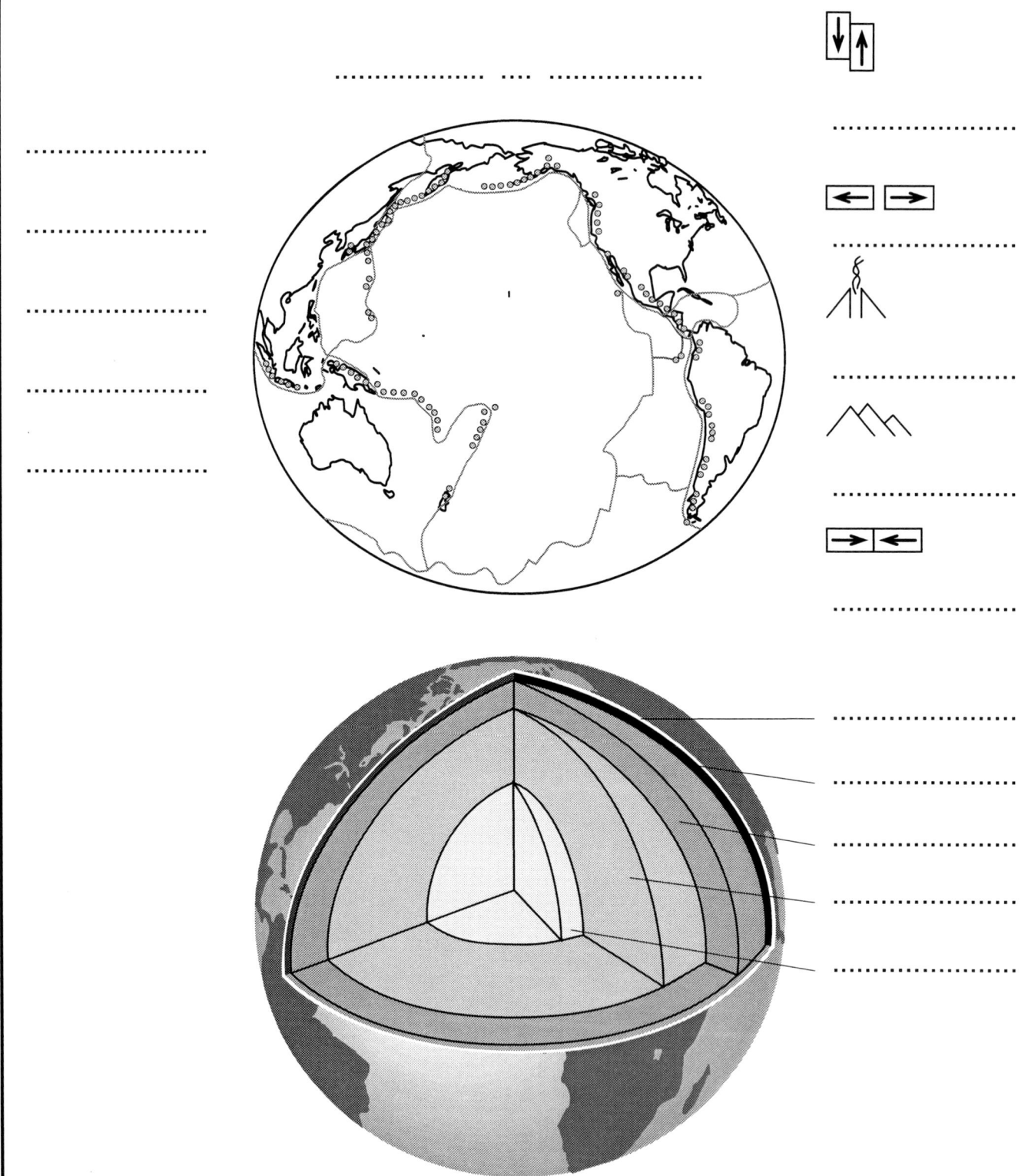

Jumbled Word-bank

epatl, lemnat, calvono, sctru, auflt, eroc, reqarutkaeh, mlou
fdotninas, thrnce, idrge, ceaonic, oncintalten, nneri, terou,
ilacsd ran, frnf eg ioir

Volcanic activity

Objective:

To understand what happens when a volcano erupts.

Teaching point:

This activity allows the students to reinforce prior learning and places emphasis on key words.

What you will need:
Copies of Copymaster 2.2.

Time:
10 minutes

Key words: lava, magma, chamber, dormant, active, extinct, pyroclastic, "Ring of Fire"

Activity:

a) Give out Copymaster 2.2 to the students. Read through the key words as a class and explain vocabulary if necessary.

b) The students need to link the words together from the Copymaster, either individually or in pairs. The links can be made orally or by drawing lines from one box to the next. The blank boxes on the Copymaster are for the students to fill in any vital information that they need to explain the links they make. These can be written as notes or as simple diagrams.

c) The students can report back to the class if appropriate. Warning – many students will have knowledge about volcanic eruptions based on films such as "Volcano" and "Dante's Peak". Be prepared to tackle incorrect ideas.

Challenge: The students can invent hand signals to represent each of the key words and use these to tell their story.

Take it forward: The students should use the remainder of the lesson to link the key words with a real volcanic eruption. Websites such as www.mvo.ac.uk provide up-to-date information on the Montserrat volcanic eruption. Emphasis should be placed on using facts and figures wherever possible.

Volcanic activity

Extinct		"Ring of Fire"	Fault
Magma Chamber	Tectonic Plates		Volcanic Bomb
	Ash	Active	
Crater		Small Earthquakes	Mud Flows
Pyroclastic Flow	Magma		Lava
	Dormant	Hot Spot	Gas

Earthquake empathy

Objective:

To understand why large earthquakes don't necessarily cause the most deaths.

Teaching point:

The students examine the effects of a recent earthquake in a LEDC and empathise with people affected by it. This exercise will also reinforce map skills and can be linked to the literacy strategy.

What you will need:
Copies of Copymaster 2.3a base map of Algeria (enlarged to A3 preferably), Copymasters 2.3b-c news report.

Time:
10 minutes

Key words: LEDC, MEDC, corruption, epicentre

Activity:

a) Give the students Copymaster map 2.3a. Also point out the scale and compass. Tell them that you are going to read a report about an earthquake that happened in the area.

b) Read out the newspaper article from Copymasters 2.3b-c to the students. The first time, the students just listen with an explanation of key words given if necessary. These can also be added to the whiteboard.

c) Then read the article again. This time, the students add the important information from the article to their base maps. They can do this by either writing and/or drawing. It is up to them to select what information is important and what information can be discarded. Emphasis should be placed on including facts and figures.

d) The students can then put the information on their maps in categories using the key, e.g. causes, effects, primary effects, secondary effects.

Challenge: Access different newspaper reports about earthquakes or volcanic eruptions from a website or other sources. Give pairs of students different reports. Each student can then make their own annotated map or diagrams of the event, then exchange the maps. Their neighbour then has to make sense of and describe the event using only the map.

Take it forward: Students may use the remainder of the lesson to compare this earthquake with another in a MEDC, e.g. Japan, USA, looking especially at why so many people were affected by it. They could consider what could have been done to reduce the effects and explore ways in which these kinds of natural hazards could be predicted.

Badger Key Stage 3 Geography Starters

Base Map of Northern Algeria

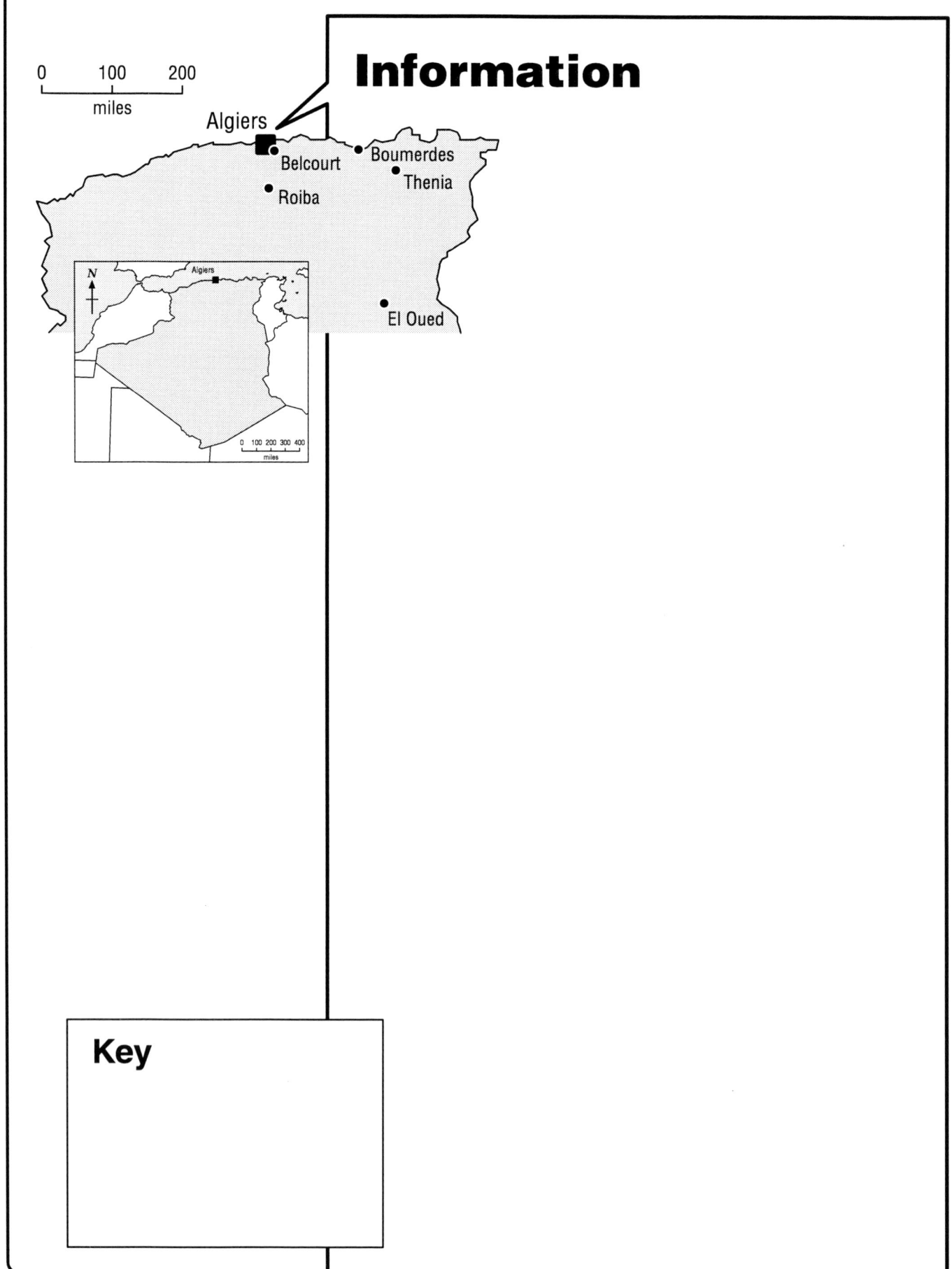

Information

Key

Disaster as they dined -
Algeria toll tops 1000

The Times – Friday May 23 2002
From Adam Sage in Paris

Families sitting down to dinner had their lives shattered in a few terrifying seconds as Algeria was hit by its most violent earthquake in two decades.

More than 1000 people died and nearly 7000 were injured as buildings were reduced to rubble along the northern coast. Thousands more are feared trapped under debris.

Screams of terror filled the night air as concrete, bricks and mortar collapsed into mounds of rubble and dust on Wednesday.

"I was on the balcony, looking at central Algiers, when I saw what looked like an enormous dust cloud" one resident said. "I went dizzy as the building began to sway back and forth like a see-saw. All the furniture fell over, the chandelier flew out of the window."

At least 57 buildings collapsed in central Algiers and nearly 100 boats were destroyed or damaged in the Balearic Islands by the ripple effect from the earthquake.

In the university town of Rouiba, on the far eastern outskirts of the capital, a three-storey faculty building simply folded in on itself. All around, houses were damaged.

Rescuers who worked through the night managed to pull a young woman, whose name was given only as Latifa, from the wreckage of the Bab-Ezzouar faculty building. When rescuers found her, only her feet were visible, and they thought she was dead. But then she called out.

"It was a miracle" said a neighbour. "They covered her legs with a blanket, and they talked to her while they pulled her free." Her husband, however, was crushed by a beam and he did not survive.

With hospitals overwhelmed and rescuers scrambling to find survivors amid the debris, Ahmed Ouyahia, the Algerian Prime Minister said "We have to expect high figures. The death toll could be revised upwards. What is still worrying is that there are still many under the rubble."

Disaster as they dined -
Algeria toll tops 1000

The epicentre of the earthquake, measured at 6.8 on the Richter scale, was in a relatively densely populated zone 64 kilometres (40 miles) east of Algiers.

The US Geological Society said that the earthquake was the biggest in Algeria since 1980, when 2,500 people died in the north-western city of Al Asnam. That was measured at 7.7 on the Richter Scale.

The tremor was felt as far away as Ibiza in Spain, where boats were damaged at their moorings.

In the worst affected town of Boumerdes, 50 kilometres (30 miles) east of the capital, a dozen apartment blocks were flattened. Thousands are feared still trapped. Towns such as Thenia, Bourmerdes and Rouiba were worst affected, with witnesses saying that many bocks of flats had collapsed. The earthquake sent thousands of people running into the street amid scenes of chaos and panic.

Many spent the night outdoors as dozens of aftershocks were felt in the region, and only returned home yesterday. There was anger among inhabitants who said that modern buildings were destroyed while older ones remained standing. They blamed unscrupulous property developers for constructing cheap, flimsy housing.

In Reghaia, a ten-storey building collapsed in a matter of seconds, according to neighbours, burying dozens on people in a mass of concrete. There were no survivors.

"Why did this one fall and not the others?" one man asked. "It's because they put in too much water when they made up the concrete - just to make a bigger profit."

Icham Mouiss, from Boumerdes, told the French television station LCI "I saw the earth tremble. I saw people jump from the window of the hotel."

Yazid Khelfaoui, whose mother was killed when her block of flats collapsed, said "I have never seen such a disaster in my life. Everything has collapsed."

Hazard detectives

Objective:

To understand the damage that earthquakes can cause.

What you will need:
An OHT of Copymaster 2.4.

Teaching point:

The students use the enquiry approach to discover some effects of an earthquake.

Time:
10 minutes

Key words: cause, effect, primary, secondary, long-term, short-term

Activity:

a) Show the students the picture on Copymaster 2.4 as a group, using an OHP or interactive whiteboard. Alternatively, this could be done as individuals, in pairs or in groups. Do not say that an earthquake caused the damage.

b) Explain to the students that they need to try and find out what has happened. In their groups, they are each allowed to ask five questions to an eyewitness. They need to start with:

What?
When?
Why?
Where?
How?

c) A representative student from each group can then pose their questions to the eyewitness (a selected student). The answers can be collated by a reporter (another selected student). Evaluate the questions to see which ones would be most likely to produce the most useful answers.

d) If appropriate, the students can discuss as a class what they think has really happened.

Challenge: For another photograph, the students can interview each other to discover what has happened.

Take it forward: The students could plot earthquakes on a world map and rank the damage caused. Are there any patterns between amount of damage, the intensity of the earthquake and the status of a country?

© Rex Features

Earthquake survival techniques

Objective:

To understand how people manage hazards.

Teaching point:

The students learn how individuals, governments and aid agencies can improve the chances of survival in an earthquake.

What you will need:
Copies of Copymasters 2.5a-d, cut into cards. Each set of cards should be photocopied in different colours.

Time:
10 minutes

Key words: predict, manage, appropriate, aftershocks, LEDC, MEDC

Activity:

a) Give out a set of cards from Copymasters 2.5a-b to each pair of students.

b) The students need to sort the cards into three groups.

   • What to do before an earthquake?

   • What to do during an earthquake?

   • What to do after an earthquake?

   Explain that people's lives can be saved by being prepared for a natural hazard, so it is vital that they put the cards in the right order!

c) Next, hand out a set of cards from Copymasters 2.5c-d to each pair of students. These should be sorted and added to the previous piles of cards as these relate to what groups (governments and aid agencies) can do, rather than individuals.

Challenge: Pairs of students can be given countries to represent, e.g. some approaches may be more appropriate in MEDCs (Japan, USA) rather than LEDCs (Turkey, Armenia).

Take it forward: The students can carry out further research into managing and coping with the effects of earthquakes. They could use the information to design a poster, website, presentation or video to show people how to cope with different kinds of natural hazards.

Individual Actions

Move away from windows.	Turn off electricity.
Arrange a meeting point with family.	Fix furniture to walls if possible.
Get a portable radio.	Protect head.
Keep away from power cables.	Place heavy items (e.g. a television) on bottom shelves.
Make first aid kit.	Do not re-enter the building.
Hang onto door frame.	Check for fire.

Earthquake survival techniques

Individual Actions

Get adequate insurance.	Keep away from trees.
Stop driving.	Get outside if possible.
Turn off gas.	Listen to the radio.
Do not panic.	Do not use matches.
Collect some food rations.	Find a torch.
Help injured people.	Go underneath a table.

Earthquake survival techniques

Group Actions

Provide first aid training.	Organise aid.
Fly in blankets.	Build power stations away from faults.
Leave areas near housing free as green areas, e.g. parks.	Give out advice via the radio.
Organise earthquake drills.	Use 'smart meters' to turn off gas.
Build housing using inflammable materials.	Monitor tremors.
Accept international aid immediately.	Identify 'safe areas' for citizens.

Earthquake survival techniques

Group Actions

Examine patterns of previous earthquakes.	Provide education programmes.
Monitor temperature of water in wells.	Bring thermal-imaging cameras and sniffer dogs.
Plan where to build houses (zoning).	Strengthen bridges.
Store and provide clean water.	Provide immunisation programme.
Monitor aftershocks.	Ensure buildings are earthquake proof.
Manage help from the army.	Use loud hailers to organise people.

Living with tectonic activity

Objective:

To understand why people live near volcanoes and areas where there are likely to be earthquakes.

What you will need:
Copies of Copymasters 2.6a-b, OHT of Copymaster 2.6c world map.

Time:
10 minutes

Teaching point:

Individuals live in hazardous areas for a variety of reasons. This activity allows the students to examine some of those reasons and to match them to an appropriate location.

Key words: cost, benefit, LEDC, MEDC, tourism, agriculture, geothermal

Activity:

a) Display Copymaster 2.6c on an overhead projector or interactive whiteboard. The students may work as individuals, in pairs or as groups for this activity.

b) Hand out Copymasters 2.6a-b and allow the students about 5 minutes to match each response to the correct location on the map.

c) Collate the students' responses and give out correct answers. Discuss the answers, paying particular attention to where people have a choice of where to live compared to those who don't have such a choice.

Answers:		
	A = Kobe, Japan	B = Iceland
	C = St Lucia	D = Naples, Italy
	E = California	F = Montserrat

Challenge: The students can plan a world tour for a group of geographers and geologists who are interested in studying earthquakes and volcanoes. Choose the top ten places they might like to visit. Briefly describe what they might see there and what they might learn.

Take it forward: As a class, examine two contrasting locations with tectonic activity, one in a LEDC and one in a MEDC. Examine why people continue to live there and research what the government does to help predict the hazard.

Living with tectonic activity

A. We have the most advanced prediction methods in the world. Although we have a lot of earthquakes, our houses have been built so that they are earthquake proof. We also have one of the best standards of living in the world with excellent schools and medical facilities.

B. I live in one of the most remote parts of the world, but it has also been called one of the most beautiful. All our energy comes from under the ground (geothermal) so we have very little pollution here. This is handy as it can get quite cold here, although we are known for swimming outside in our huge heated swimming pools.

C. We are quite a poor country, but lots of tourists come to our island to stay in our expensive hotels because we have hot weather all year round. They also spend their money visiting the hot springs in the centre of the islands and this helps to improve our roads and schools. The fertile soil also means that we grow a lot of bananas and these are exported all over the world.

D. I can see the volcano nearly all the time as it dominates the landscape of my home city and shadows nearly all the houses and the people. This volcano was due to erupt nearly thirty years ago but we are still waiting. When it erupted in AD79, two whole cities and their people were buried underneath. Luckily, the last time it erupted in 1944, the lava was diverted towards the sea. This is the most monitored volcano in the world.

E. We think we live in one of the most hazardous places in the world. We have big earthquakes every one hundred years. The last big one killed 60 people when a double-decker freeway fell over. We have one of the highest crime rates in our country and have experienced some of the worst riots in living memory. House insurance is either impossible to get or very expensive. I'd like to move but most jobs are here as it's a national and international centre for entertainment.

F. I was evacuated from my home to the UK in 1996 when a volcano erupted. We weren't prepared at all as we didn't even know that there was a volcano on our island – we thought it was a hill! The ash was so bad that we had to wear masks at school so we didn't breath it in. We didn't want to move so far away, but people in the UK were the only ones who would help us.

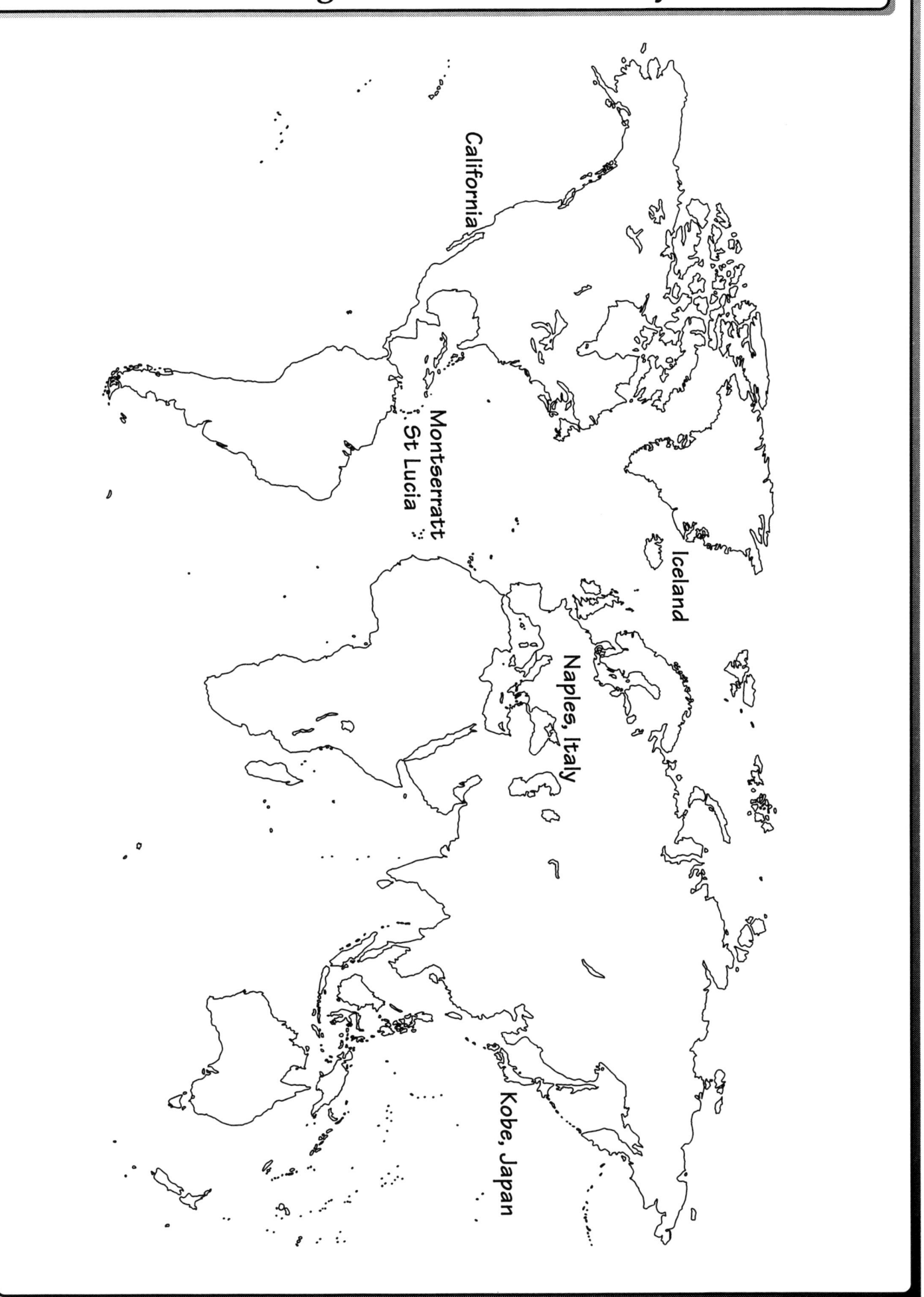

California

Montserratt
St Lucia

Iceland

Naples, Italy

Kobe, Japan

Quality of life

Objective:

To provide a starting point for further discussion about quality of life in MEDCs and LEDCs.

What you will need:
Sets of cards from Copymaster 3.1.

Time:
5-10 minutes

Teaching point:

This activity is designed to be used as an introduction to a unit of work on 'Measuring wealth'. It aims to develop an understanding that quality of life is subjective by starting with the students' own perceptions of indices of wealth and poverty. This material needs to be handled with sensitivity in the classroom.

Key words: quality of life, MEDC, LEDC, development

Activity:

a) Students should work in pairs for this activity. Give each pair of students the statements from Copymaster 3.1 (already cut up).

b) They are to 'diamond rank' the statements according to factors they think are most important to a good quality of life, i.e. the most important factor, then the next two important factors, followed by the next three, until the least important factor. The statements should form the following pattern:

```
            1
        2       3
    4       5       6
        7       8
            9
```

c) There are 14 statements, therefore the students do not have to use all of them. The students should also be reassured that there are no right or wrong answers, but they may be asked to explain the choices they have made.

d) The feedback from pairs should be used to generate discussion on what constitutes a 'good' quality of life and how it may differ from person to person.

Challenge: The students could add their own factors if there are others they deem more important to them. They could also suggest particular brands that might indicate variations in wealth.

Take it forward: This activity can be used as an introduction to measuring development and making comparisons between countries. The students could write their own factors that they think people living in a LEDC would feel constitute a 'good' quality of life.

Quality of life

Owning a car	Food
Owning a home	Good health
A good job	A university degree
Electricity	A good social life
Earning lots of money	Owning a computer
A stable family life	Good clothes
Friends	Holidays abroad

Money, money, money

Objective:

To provide a starting point for discussion about using GNP as a measure of development.

Teaching point:

The students should come to appreciate that economic wealth is not necessarily either the only or the best sign of development.

What you will need:
An OHT of Copymaster 3.2.

Time:
5 minutes

Key words: wealth, development, GNP per capita, LEDC, MEDC

Activity:

a) Display OHT 3.2, a list of countries. Stress to the students that the countries are in no particular order.

b) Students are to rank the countries in order they think are the richest to the poorest.

c) Feedback. Students share their answers.

- Are there similarities or differences in their responses?

- What criteria did they use for deciding on whether a country was rich or not?

- Where did they get the knowledge from?

- Is it knowledge they've learnt at school, seen on the news, from film, first-hand experiences, etc?

Challenge: Students compare their ranks with those of a neighbour, then use an atlas to put the countries in order from highest GNP per capita to lowest. How do the two lists compare?

Take it forward: The starter could be used to generate discussion on using GNP as a measure of development. It might be useful to discuss other factors that we would associate with a 'developed' country, e.g. high literacy levels, and use a country such as Saudi Arabia to illustrate the fact that a reasonable GNP per capita isn't necessarily an indicator of a good quality of life for all the people or that there is a high level of development in all parts of a country.

Money, money, money

Australia	UK
Germany	India
USA	Kenya
Brazil	Egypt
Japan	Bangladesh
Tanzania	Spain
Mozambique	Peru
New Zealand	Ethiopia
Zimbabwe	Sweden
Switzerland	South Africa

Challenging stereotypes

Objective:

To challenge any stereotypes and pre-conceived ideas the students may have about LEDCs and MEDCs.

Teaching point:

National data and maps on a global scale tend to hide inequalities in wealth within both MEDCs and LEDCs. The students should also be made aware that the limited selection of photos often used in text books can represent an unbalanced and distorted view of reality. They need to be made aware that complexity is a key feature of the levels and distribution of wealth in most countries.

What you will need:
An OHT of Copymaster 3.3.

Time:
10 minutes

Key words: MEDC, LEDC, wealth, inequality, rich, poor, development

Activity:

a) Introduce the activity to the students. They are to examine the four images shown in Copymaster 3.3 and decide whether the image shows an MEDC or an LEDC. This activity is probably best done in pairs to enable some discussion to take place. The students are to justify their choices.

b) For feedback, select students to share their answers with the class. Ask them to justify the choice they made.

  • Why do they think the image is an LEDC or MEDC?

  • What features are shown on the images that made them think this?

  • Are the students surprised by any of the actual locations?

The images show:

  A = Johannesburg, South Africa

  B = Homeless person on streets of New York

  C = Masai Mara, Kenya

  D = UK rubbish tip

Challenge: The students could write a paragraph to explain how their perceptions of LEDCs and MEDCs has changed (if at all).

Take it forward: This starter could be used to lead into a lesson on regional inequalities in wealth within MEDCs or LEDCs, using case study material to add appropriate detail.

Challenging stereotypes

Development dominoes

Objective:

To assess the use of selected indices of development as indicators of the quality of life in a variety of countries.

Teaching point:

The statistics present the students with both an index of economic wealth and with indices of quality of life. An aim is to reflect on how closely they are linked and to begin to consider reasons for links between them.

What you will need:
Sets of cards from Copymaster 3.4.

Time:
10 minutes

Key words: wealth, GDP per capita, literacy rate, life expectancy, LEDC, MEDC

Activity:

Before the lesson, photocopy Copymaster 3.4 and cut up the cards. (This could always be used as a whole class activity if the Copymaster was photocopied onto an OHT and then cut up). The GDP per capita figures have been adjusted to reflect Purchasing Power Parity. All the statistics are taken from the CIA World Factbook. www.cia.gov/cia/publications/factbook

a) Hand out the cards to students. They could work in pairs or small groups for this activity. Tell the students that the aim of the activity is to match the statistics provided to the countries. It may be necessary to spend a few minutes discussing the meaning of GDP per capita, literacy rate and life expectancy. This is also an opportunity to discuss how literacy rate and life expectancy are indicators of quality of life (access to healthcare, education systems, etc).

b) Students feedback their answers. This should facilitate discussion on the relationship between wealth and quality of life.

Challenge: Using an atlas, students could locate the countries on a world map and describe any spatial patterns they notice.

Take it forward: This starter could be used to introduce a lesson on the relationship between wealth and quality of life.

Development dominoes

GDP per capita $25,300	UK	Literacy Rate 99% Life Expectancy 78.0 years
GDP per capita $36,300	USA	Literacy Rate 97% Life Expectancy 77.4 years
GDP per capita $27,000	Australia	Literacy Rate 100% Life Expectancy 80 years
GDP per capita $1,750	Bangladesh	Literacy Rate 56% Life Expectancy 60.9 years
GDP per capita $9,400	South Africa	Literacy Rate 85% Life Expectancy 45.4 years
GDP per capita $700	Ethiopia	Literacy Rate 35.5% Life Expectancy 44.2 years

Stepping into a photograph

Objective:

To provide a basis for further discussion about the quality of life for some people living in LEDCs.

Teaching point:

To consider what life would be like living below the poverty line.

What you will need:
An OHT of Copymaster 3.5.

Time:
10 minutes

Key words: poverty, LEDC, shanty town, squatter settlement, sanitation, shelter, migration, life expectancy, wealth, employment, quality of life

Activity:

a) Show the students an OHT of Copymaster 3.5. For the first few minutes, ask them to 'step into' the photograph and adopt the role of one of the people shown. The choice could be left open to the students or they could be directed towards one of the characters who might ideally be someone of a similar age to themselves. The students should then begin the activity by writing down what they imagine their character to be thinking at the moment the photograph was taken. They could then share their thoughts with partners or as part of a whole class feedback session.

b) The students should then 'step out' of the photograph and, as themselves, write down questions they would like to ask their character.

c) For group feedback discuss these questions:

- Have the students asked similar sorts of questions?

- How do they think their life differs from the person in the photograph?

- Do they think the person has a good quality of life?

- Does the person appear to be happy?

Challenge: The students could write a day in the life of their character from the photograph. What do they think daily life is like for that person? What tasks do they think that person has to perform each day?

Take it forward: The remainder of the lesson might consist of a case study of a squatter settlement and examine issues such as rural-urban migration and the associated push and pull factors.

© Rex Features

Search for the truth

Objective:

To draw together the students' thinking on 'Measuring wealth' and development issues.

Teaching point:

This starter aims to generate discussion and get students justifying their opinions. It should be used at the end of a unit of work on development or 'Measuring wealth' as it relies on students' existing knowledge.

What you will need:
An OHT of Copymaster 3.6, or sets of cards from it.

Time:
5-10 minutes

Key words: development, wealth, quality of life, MEDC, LEDC, poverty, GDP, life expectancy, aid

Activity:

a) The 10 statements could either be displayed on an OHT or cut up and given to pairs or small groups.

b) The students are to classify the statements as either Fact (where evidence could be provided to support the statement), Fiction (completely untrue), or Opinion (could be right or wrong). These terms may need to be explained to the students. Stress that there are no answers that are strictly right or wrong, but that they will be expected to explain the choices they make.

c) For feedback, take each statement in turn and select students to say whether they thought the statement was Fact, Fiction or Opinion. The students should then be asked to justify the choice they made. At this point others could be asked for their opinions.

Challenge: Students could write statements of their own to fit each of the three columns, Fact, Fiction and Opinion.

Take it forward: This starter could be used to introduce a revision or summary lesson on development and the indices used to measure wealth.

Search for the truth

GDP per capita is a good indicator of quality of life.	Life expectancy is a good indicator of quality of life.
There are more people living in MEDCs than LEDCs.	Poverty only exists in LEDCs.
All people in MEDCs are rich.	Wealthy people are happier than poorer people.
Most countries have some very wealthy and some very poor people.	People in LEDCs want aid from people in MEDCs.
Everyone has the right to food, clean water and shelter.	LEDCs should follow the example set by MEDCs.

The African savannah ecosystem

Objective:

Students will develop an understanding of African savannah ecosystems.

Teaching point:

By using a diagram as a stimulus, together with a simple concept map, students can develop an understanding of the interconnections of an ecosystem.

What you will need:
An OHT of Copymaster 4.1a, A3 copies of Copymaster 4.1b and the statements on Copymaster 4.1c, envelopes for these statements.

Time:
12 minutes

Key words: ecosystems, sparsely populated, densely populated, prevailing wind, nomadic herding, overgrazing, over-cultivation, deforestation, interconnections

Activity:

a) Introduce the concept of a system with reference to an engine, a computer or the human body. Develop the idea that different parts in the system are linked to make the whole thing work. Ask the students for some of their own examples.

b) Then introduce the word 'ecosystem' by first exploring their understanding of the common contexts in which the word 'eco' is used, for example, as in 'eco-friendly' for washing up liquid. Develop the idea by explaining that ecology is the study of natural living systems.

c) Then show students an OHT of Copymaster 4.1a. Ask the students to describe what they are looking at, then use evidence to guess where in the world they think the place is.

d) Provide the students with Copymaster 4.1b. Working in pairs or threes, ask them to identify the parts of the diagram on the picture. They should also explain the arrows.

e) Provide each group of students with an envelope with Copymaster 4.1c cut up into 9 statements. Then ask them to place the statements on the diagram in places that will show how the different parts of the system are linked.

Challenge: The same activity as above can be made more challenging by removing the arrows from Copymaster 4.1b. The students could also look for other connections, i.e. how the soil influences human activity or how humans might be influencing the climate in this ecosystem.

Take it forward: The students could reinforce their learning about ecosystems with a role-play activity. Volunteers could take on the role of climate, i.e. the sun and rain. Other students could be trees. Some students might be wildebeest, lions and hyenas. This could be followed by studies of other ecosystems that the students choose for themselves. They should use the headings on the concept map (without the arrows) to find out about other ecosystems, e.g. tropical rainforests, deserts, tundra, temperate forests.

The African savannah ecosystem

The African savannah ecosystem

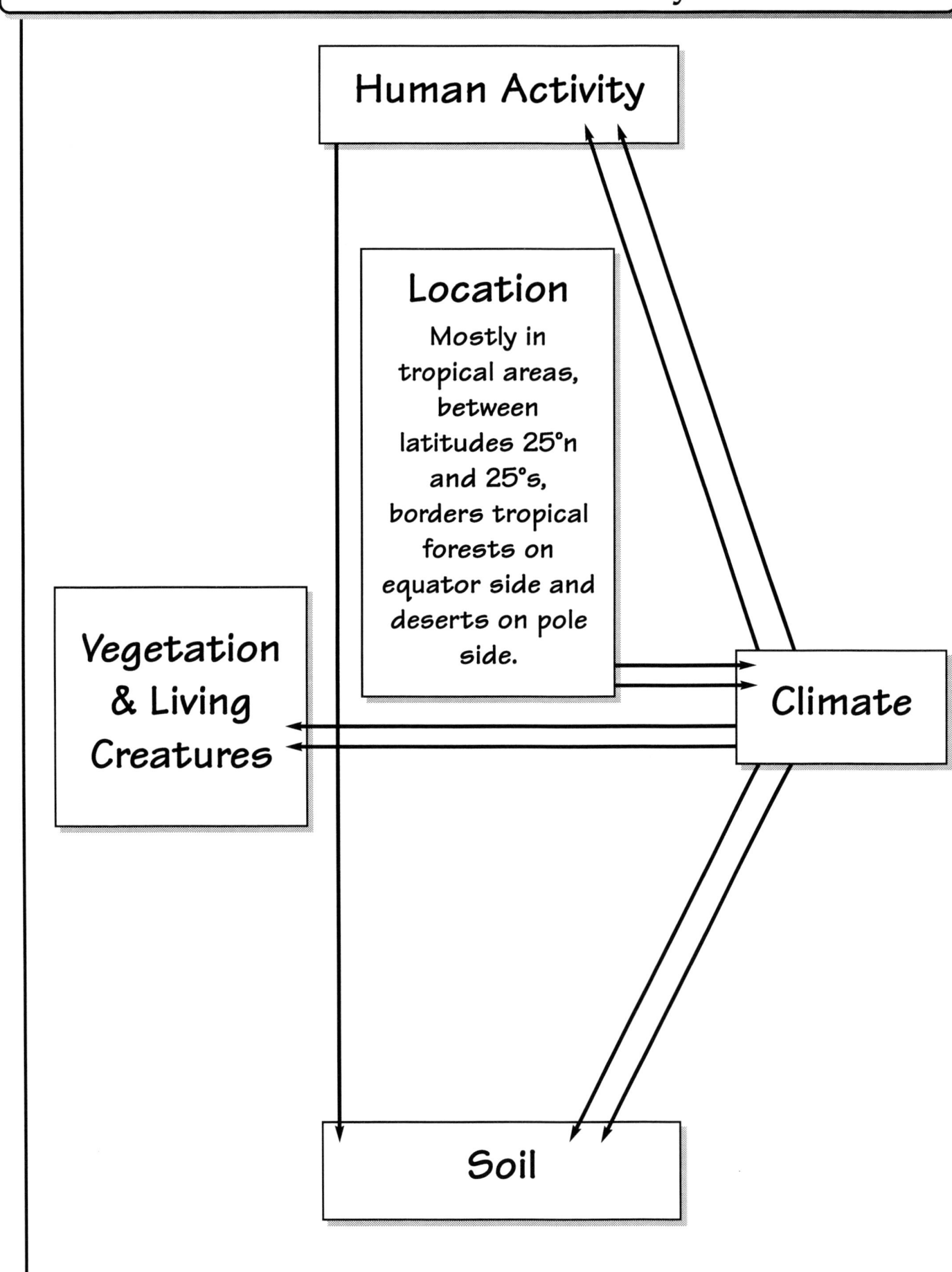

The African savannah ecosystem

A. Has a wet season due to it being close to the equator. The prevailing wind changes direction and brings heavy rain which would usually fall nearer the equator.

B. High population growth due to high birth and reduced death rates. As a result more animals and more crops are needed, leading to overgrazing, over-cultivation and deforestation. This leads to soil erosion and some areas turn to desert.

C. Soil at risk of turning to desert because of dry and hot conditions for most of the year.

D. Hot throughout the year because of being close to the equator. The sun's rays are more concentrated nearer the equator.

E. It's too dry and not wet enough for large forests so it's mostly grassland, with scattered trees.

F. Seasonal, nomadic herding to provide new grass for animals during the dry season.

G. During the wet season may have nutrients washed out and during the dry season may form a hard crust.

H. Trees, bushes and grasses have to adapt to the climate. The Baobab tree, for example, has a huge trunk which stores water.

I. The area is sparsely populated because it is a difficult environment in which to survive. It is mostly hot and dry and the farming conditions difficult.

Soil ~ time to get your fingers dirty

Objective:

The students will learn about the basic characteristics of soils and their importance.

Teaching point:

This is a difficult topic in which to stimulate the student's interests. By creating a mystery out of it, interest and motivation may be raised.

What you will need:
An OHT of Copymaster 4.2.

Time:
5 minutes

Key words: soil, humus, fertilise, leached

Activity:

a) Tell the students that they will have to guess what topic they are going to study by looking at a set of statements. Don't tell them that soil is the topic.

b) Using an OHT of Copymaster 4.2, reveal the first clue. Take a few students' answers and then move on. The clues should become more obvious further down the list.

c) Repeat the process of unravelling the clues one at a time, leaving the previous clues on the screen, until a student guesses the correct answer.

d) Reveal all the clues if they have not already been revealed.

e) Ask students why this is a topic that geographers study. They should be able to use the clues for ideas.

Challenge: Ask students to generate some additional clues and decide where they might go in the list.

Take it forward: This could be an introduction to looking at different soils around the world, or issues to do with soil erosion or contrasting different methods of farming, e.g. organic against more intensive, industrial methods of farming.

1. It takes a long time to form ~ often 1000 years to produce 1cm.

2. Without it, there would be no animal or human life.

3. There are many different types. It varies according to texture, depth, colour, acidity and organic content.

4. It can be eroded away and its goodness leached out.

5. Dead plant and animal life help form a dark humus in it.

6. Humans can alter it by farming.

7. Farmers fertilise it.

8. Gardeners get it under their finger nails.

9. It is a thin layer, usually less than 1 metre in depth, which lies on the Earth's surface.

10. It is essential for plants and crops to grow in.

World's major ecosystems

Objective:

The students learn about the distribution of the world's major ecosystems.

Teaching point:

Students are often asked to map the distribution of the world's major ecosystems. This activity offers a different approach to that task.

What you will need:

A3 copies of Copymasters 4.3a (ecosystem map) and 4.3b (student outline map).

Time:
10 minutes

Key words: ecosystem, biomes, distribution

Activity:

a) Organise the students into pairs. Give each pair a copy of Copymasters 4.3a and 4.3b. Tell the students that they will work competitively, in pairs, to reproduce aspects of 4.3a onto 4.3b. Allow the students one minute to look at both maps.

b) One student takes Copymaster 4.3a and the other student takes Copymaster 4.3b. The student with the outline map should not be able to see the ecosystem map. The teacher selects an ecosystem. The student with the ecosystem map has 2 minutes to describe the location of the selected ecosystem to the other student who has to draw and label it.

c) The students then change roles. The process is repeated for a second ecosystem. Continue until 4 ecosystems have been completed.

d) Ask the students to compare the map they have drawn to the ecosystem map. Ask them to evaluate their success at drawing the map and to suggest why some maps might be better than others.

Challenge: Ask students to write accurate descriptions of the distributions of selected ecosystems.

Take it forward: Ask the students to identify any patterns in the distribution of the various ecosystems. The students should then examine the reasons for the differing distributions of the different ecosystems.

World's major ecosystems

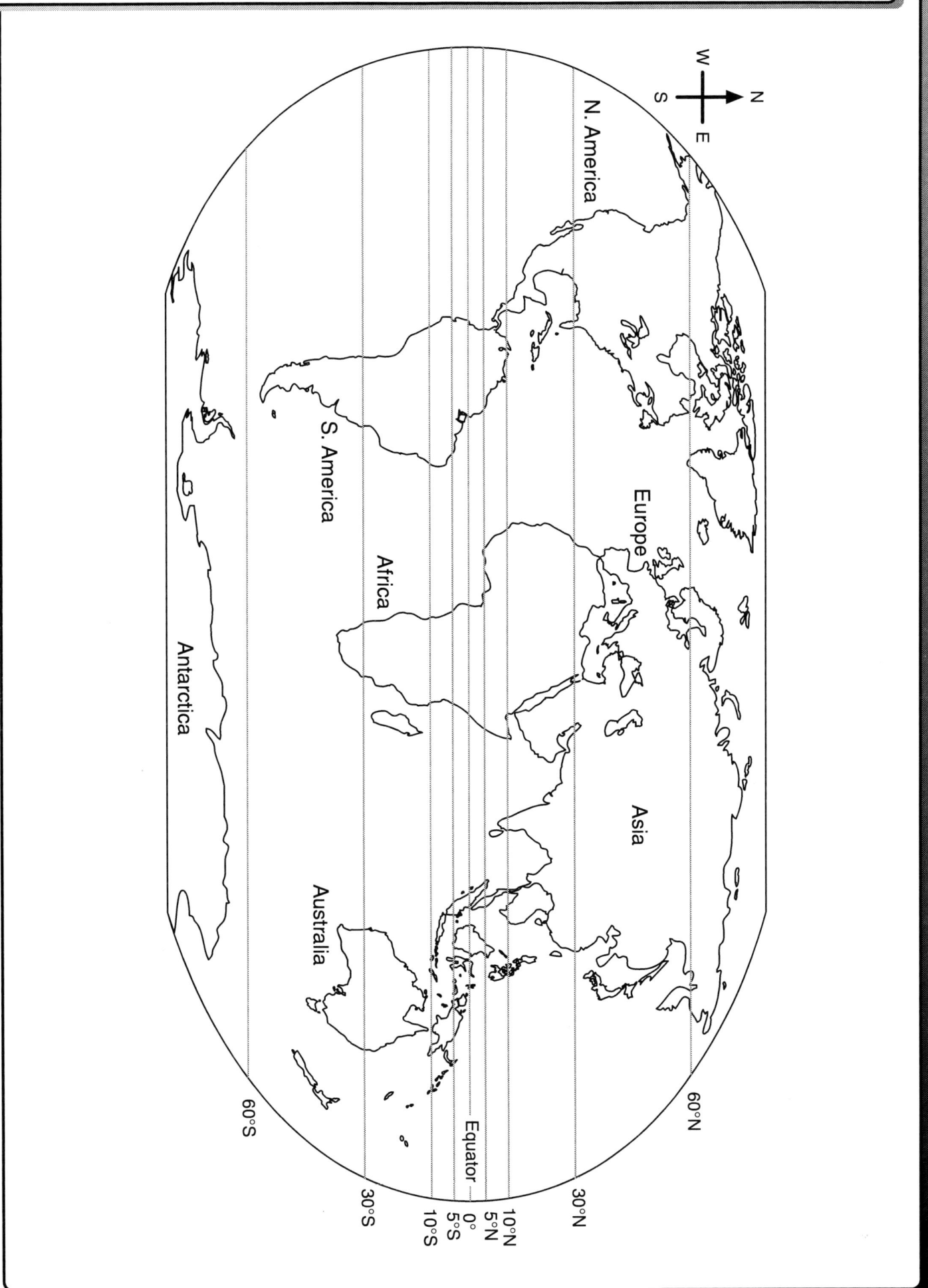

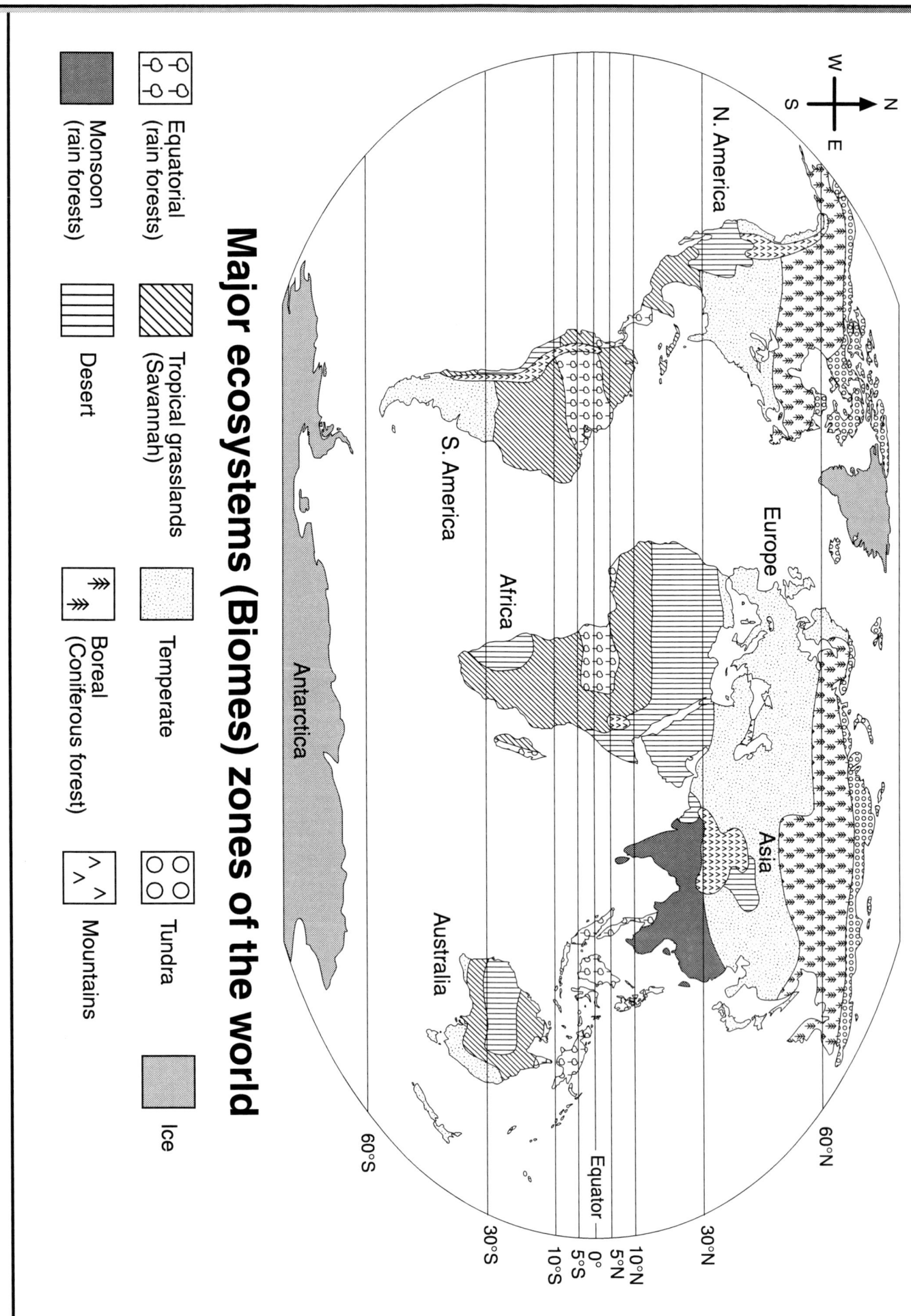

Major ecosystems (Biomes) zones of the world

Legend:

- Equatorial (rain forests)
- Monsoon (rain forests)
- Tropical grasslands (Savannah)
- Desert
- Temperate
- Tundra
- Boreal (Coniferous forest)
- Mountains
- Ice

Map labels: N. America, S. America, Antarctica, Africa, Europe, Asia, Australia

Latitude lines: 60°S, 30°S, 10°S, 5°S, 0° Equator, 5°N, 10°N, 30°N, 60°N

Compass: N, E, S, W

Climate and ecosystems

Objective:

Students will learn about the climate and other aspects of equatorial rainforests and desert ecosystems through the interpretation of climate graphs.

What you will need:

A3 enlarged copies of Copymaster 4.4a, copies of Copymasters 4.4b-c, envelopes, spare cards.

Time:
10 minutes

Teaching point:

It would be helpful if the students are familiar with climate graphs and the difficulties of using them.

Key words: transpiration, dormant, wadi, sparsely populated, densely populated

Activity:

a) The students work in groups of two or three. Provide each group with enlarged A3 copies of Copymaster 4.4a, showing two different climate graphs. Ask the students what the graphs show. Draw their attention to the different scales and the key.

b) Provide each group with an envelope with the statements from Copymasters 4.4b-c cut up and placed inside. The students will have to place each statement next to the most relevant climate graph. Tell the students that they will have to explain their answers.

NB: Graph A is from Adras, Algeria, and Graph B is from Manaus, Brazil.

Challenge: Provide the students with some spare cards and ask them to create their own statements relevant to the climate graphs.

Take it forward: For both ecosystems, the students could consider how climate affects the vegetation, living creatures, soil, and human activity. They could also examine the reasons why these climates are different.

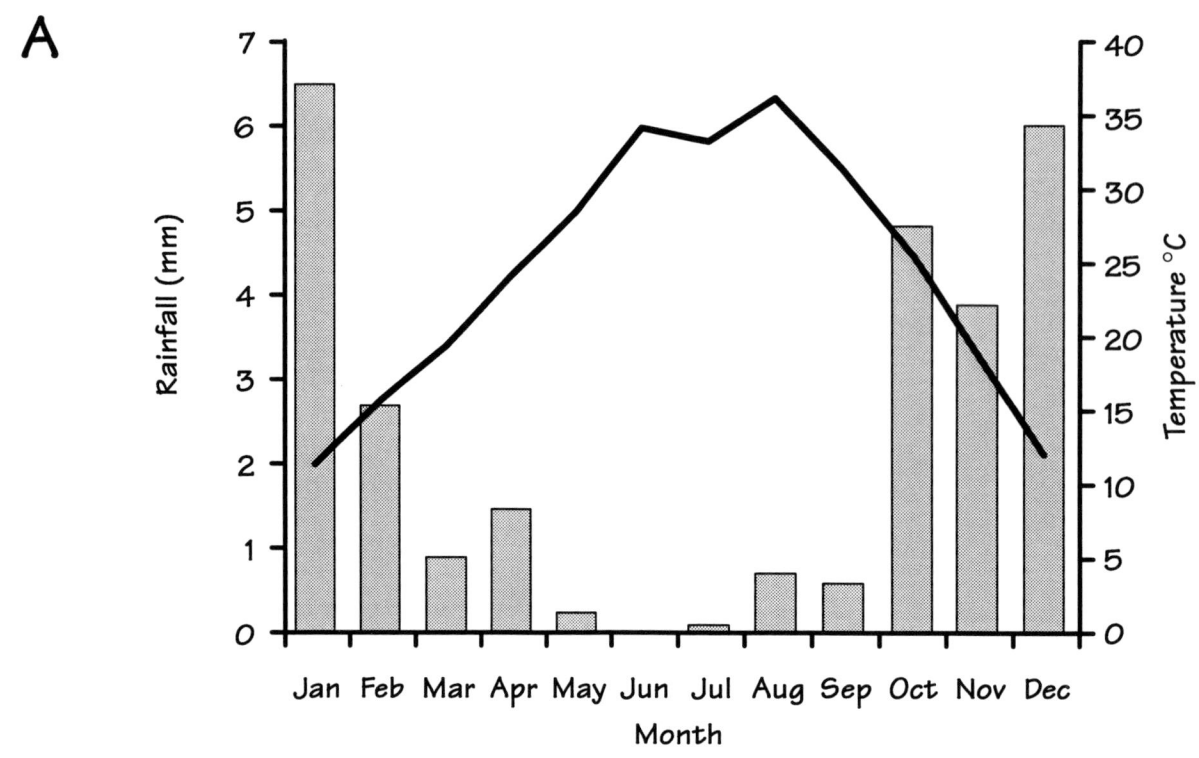

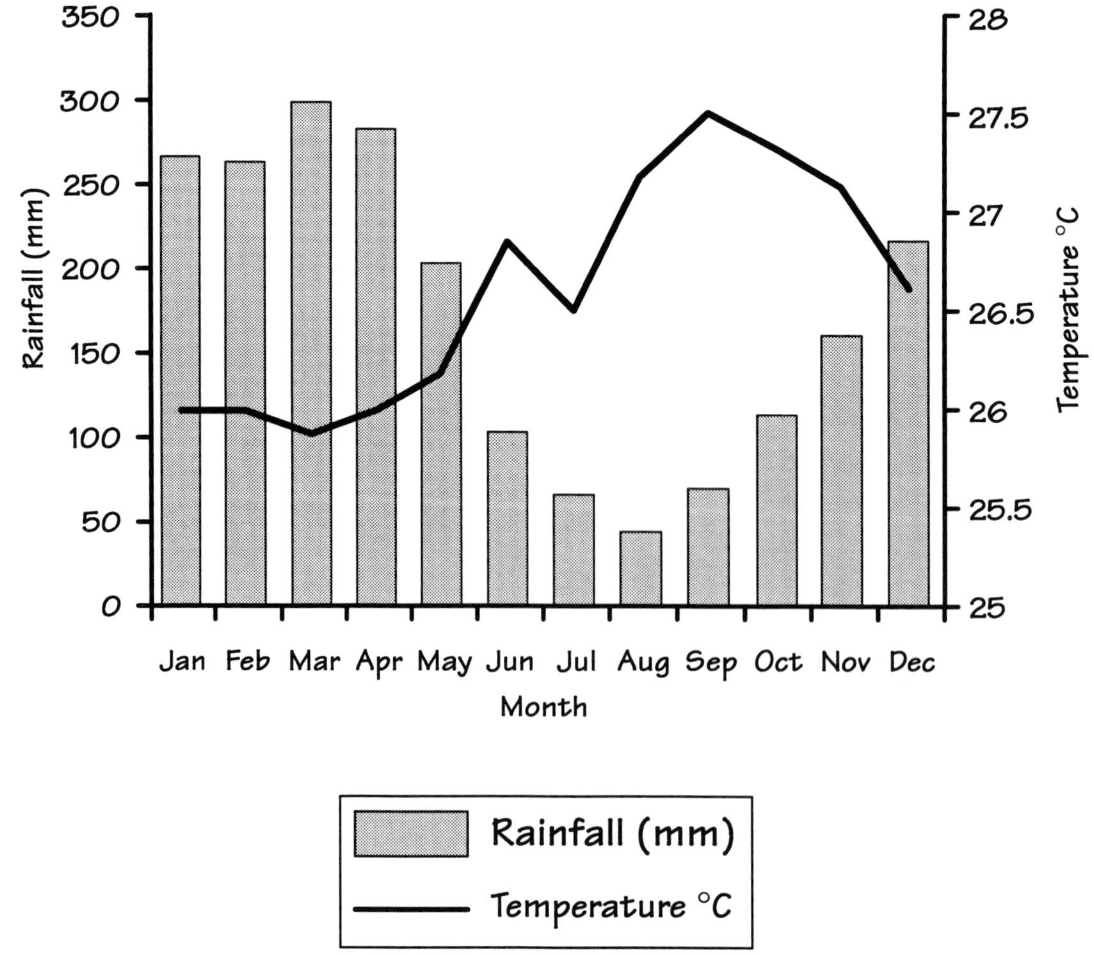

Climate and ecosystems

1. Does not rain throughout the year.

2. Lots of vegetation.

3. Desert.

4. Wet season.

5. Plants may have spikes to reduce transpiration.

6. Continuous growing season.

7. On or very close to the equator.

8. Temperatures remain similar throughout the year.

9. Flooding likely to occur.

Climate and ecosystems

10. Plant seeds may lie dormant for long periods, waiting for rainfall to enable them to flower.

11. Some rivers may dry up, forming wadis.

12. Soil can be easily washed away if trees are removed.

13. Trees grow very tall.

14. Equatorial Rainforests (Tropical Rainforests)

15. Plants have adapted to store water.

16. Sparsely populated because of a shortage of water and the harsh conditions it creates.

17. Found further from the equator, where the air is descending for most of the year. This creates high pressure and dry conditions.

Human impacts on ecosystems

Objective:
The students will learn about the impacts humans have on different ecosystems.

Teaching point:
This is a challenging task that assumes some prior knowledge. Some terms will require explaining to students.

What you will need:
Copies of Copymaster 4.5, cut up and put into envelopes, blank A4 paper.

Time:
10 minutes

Key words: over fishing, genetically modified crops, insecticide, wetlands, deforestation

Activity:

a) Ask students to work in pairs or threes. On a blank A4 piece of paper, students turn it to landscape format and draw a line across the middle of the page. They then label the right end 'No impact' and the left end 'Very severe impact'. Ask the students what are the meanings of these two terms.

b) Ask the students to empty the contents of the envelopes onto their desks and ask them if they need help understanding any of the terms. The teacher might write the meanings of these terms on the board.

c) Working in their pairs or threes, tell the students to position the cards along the line of the 'impact continuum', according to the extent they think each impact has on ecosystems. Tell the students that you will ask them to explain their positioning afterwards.

d) Whilst students are undertaking the exercise, monitor the conversations so that you can incorporate them into the debrief.

e) Ask students to feedback, providing explanations for their positionings.

Challenge: Ask students to generate other examples of human impacts on ecosystems. Students then have to write these examples on the impact continuum and explain their positionings.

Take it forward: This task can be used as part of a series of lessons on the impact that humans have on ecosystems or as an introduction to examining one of them in detail.

Human impacts on ecosystems

1. Gardening	6. Removing hedgerows between fields
2. Oil spill	7. Deforestation
3. Over fishing	8. Drainage of wetlands
4. Industrial pollution in rivers	9. Whaling
5. Growing genetically modified crops	10. Insecticide spraying on farm crops

Coral reef ecosystems

Objective:

Students will learn about the impact that tourist pressure is having on delicate coral reef ecosystems.

What you will need:
An OHT of Copymaster 4.6.

Time:
5 minutes

Teaching point:

Coral reefs are ecosystems that can provide a different and extremely colourful case study of both natural processes and of how people can affect their environment. It would be interesting to compare the processes in coral reefs with those of a tropical rain forest, perhaps in different years so that a progression of key ideas could be developed.

Key words: biodiversity, coral reefs, management, honey pot

Activity:

a) Show the students Copymaster 4.6. Ask them to explain the meaning of the cartoon.

b) Ask the students to explain the meaning of biodiversity. This may need to be done before the first activity, depending on the ability of the group.

c) Ask the students why humans are putting pressure on the coral reefs and its biodiversity.

d) Ask the students who might use a cartoon like this.

Challenge: Ask the students to think up an alternative caption for the cartoon which illustrates their understanding of what is happening.

Take it forward: Ask the students if they agree with the ideas in the cartoon. Are there any other points of view on how humans use or impact upon coral reef ecosystems? The students could also examine the distribution and formation of coral reefs. They could explore the ways in which coral reef biodiversity can be better managed.

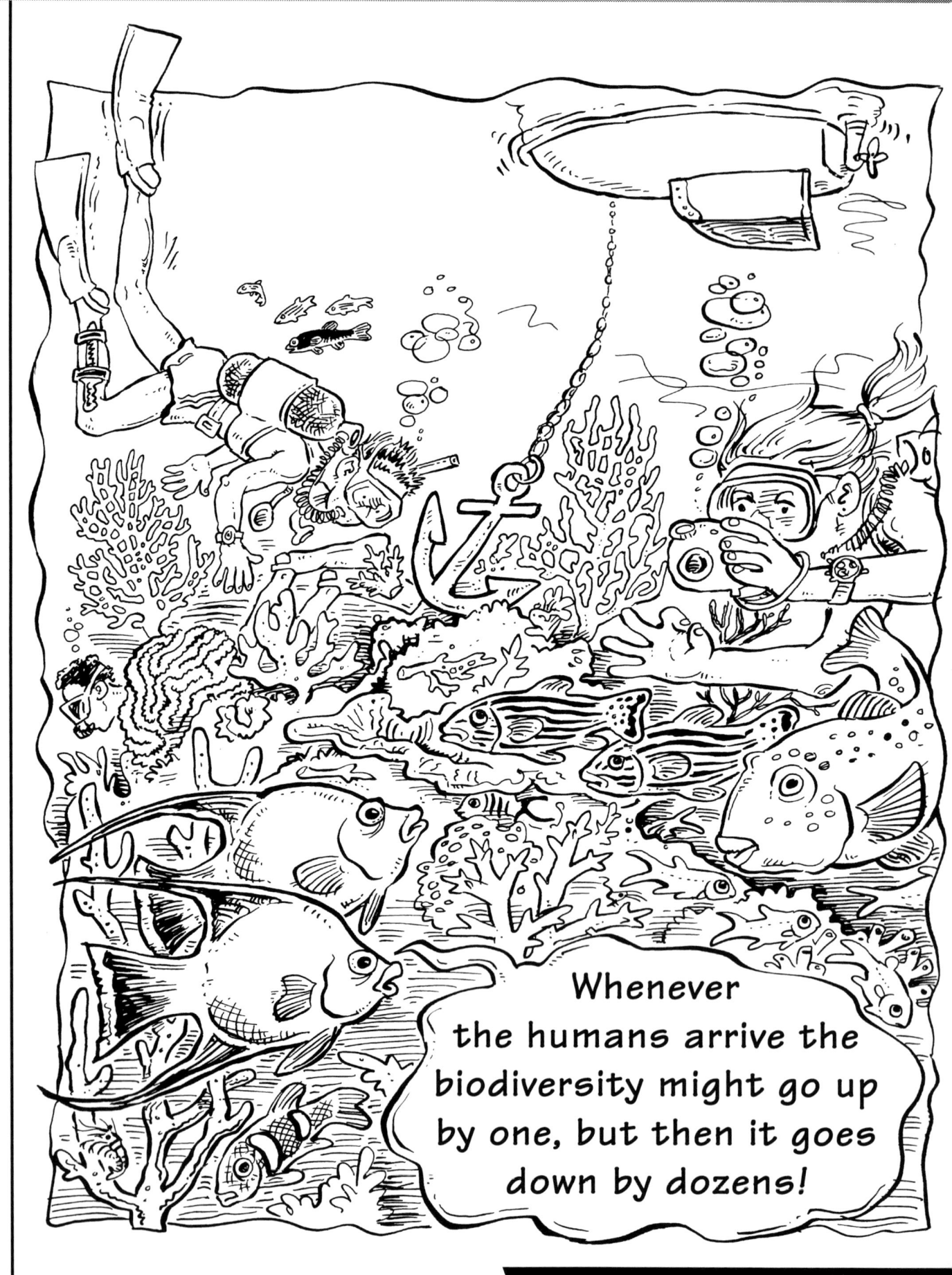

Thinking about people

Objective:

To consider the validity of evidence in relation to data and information about population.

What you will need:
Copies of Copymaster 5.1.

Time:
10 minutes

Teaching point:

Students may come to this topic with a variety of misconceptions based on partial knowledge of facts and on opinions they have heard from others. The focus of the activity is to consider some of the problems in sorting out fact from opinion, what is true from what is false.

Key words: population, resources

Activity:

a) Give out the set of cards on Copymaster 5.1. Tell the students to sort them into two piles. One pile is for statements that give facts. The other pile is for statements that are opinions. If they are unsure of any statements, they could put them separately on the side. Tell them that they are not being asked whether the facts are true or false. After the activity, you could discuss with the students whether a fact can ever be false.

b) Discuss the statements.

   • Which ones were easy to classify as fact?

   • Which were easy to classify as opinion?

   • Which ones were not so easy to classify, and why?

c) Tell the students to look at the cards that state facts. For each item, write a statement about how important this fact might be and why it might be important.

d) Discuss what the students have written. A key point to explore is the meaning of 'important', e.g. to whom might it be important, the scale of the issue, the location of the issue.

Challenge: Students should find at least two different references to check whether the facts on the cards are accurate. They can do this using websites or reference books.

Take it forward: This activity opens up ideas about world population growth and the balance of population to resources. The students could carry out further research into population data to see how to check on facts and how specific facts need to be set in their wider context.

Badger Key Stage 3 Geography Starters

Thinking about people

A. There are far too many people living in the world today.

B. The population in most countries in the world is going up quickly.

C. There will be about twice as many people living in countries in Africa in 40 years time.

D. There are about 58 million people in the UK.

E. The number of people in the UK is about right for its size and resources.

F. There are not enough people living in some countries.

G. In some countries of Asia, up to half the people are under the age of 15.

H. People are living longer in the UK than in the past.

I. People should only have children when they are rich enough to look after them.

J. The population in a country is likely to go up if there are more births each year than deaths.

The population clock

Objective:

To know that the Earth's population is increasing and to make predictions as to what it is likely to be in the future.

Teaching point:

Students find it difficult to attach real meaning to figures that are in millions and beyond. Time is also a difficult concept to understand. Relating numbers and time to the students' own number and time experiences may help them to develop a better understanding of these concepts.

What you will need:
A calculator, population data on Copymaster 5.2 (repeated twice for convenience).

Time:
10 minutes

Key words: population, births, deaths, natural increase

Activity:

a) Show students the chart of population data on Copymaster 5.2. Explain that the figures show the number of births, deaths and the increase over different time scales in the world. They can use a calculator to work out these figures:

- How many births there are every five seconds.

- How many deaths there are every five seconds.

- The world's population increase every five seconds.

- The world's population increase by the end of the lesson.

b) Ask the students to think of some times and numbers that they are familiar with that could make the population data meaningful. They can describe or illustrate at least three ideas. As an example, in the time that it takes them to run 100 metres (about 13 seconds), there would be an extra 53 births. For numbers, they could think about how many people are in their class, their primary and secondary school, their town, at a football match, and other ideas. For time scales, they could think about the length of a television programme, their school day, their next birthday, a sports event and other ideas.

c) Share these ideas when they have finished, perhaps as part of a wall display.

Challenge: Find the names of some UK cities that have population totals of 200,000 or more, i.e. the world population natural increase every day.

Take it forward: These ideas can be used to introduce students to death rates, birth rates and natural increase. They can find out about data for different countries and how the rates are changing. The students can study online population clocks such as the one at http://www.ibiblio.org/lunarbin/worldpop.

World population change in 2003

TIME UNIT	BIRTHS	DEATHS	NATURAL INCREASE
YEAR	128,746,122	55,660,746	73,085,376
MONTH	10,728,844	4,638,396	6,090,448
DAY	352,729	152,495	200,234
HOUR	14,697	6,354	8,343
MINUTE	245	106	139
SECOND	4.1	1.8	2.3

TIME UNIT	BIRTHS	DEATHS	NATURAL INCREASE
YEAR	128,746,122	55,660,746	73,085,376
MONTH	10,728,844	4,638,396	6,090,448
DAY	352,729	152,495	200,234
HOUR	14,697	6,354	8,343
MINUTE	245	106	139
SECOND	4.1	1.8	2.3

People count

Objective:

To use a graph to show the trend and amount of world population change and consider how appropriate the style of graph might be to show this data.

Teaching point:

With the use of ICT, students can now choose to show data by using a wide range of styles of graph. This makes it especially important that they are able to make appropriate choices between the different styles.

What you will need:
Copies of Copymaster 5.3.

Time:
5 minutes

Key words: line graph, population, prediction, trend

Activity:

a) Give the students the graph of world population change on Copymaster 5.3. Note the time period of 100 years and explain that figures for the future can be predicted with at least some degree of accuracy based on past and present trends. Also note the figures in billions (US).

b) They can use the graph to work out the world's population at the different years shown on the Copymaster. Review the figures they work out. Emphasise the trend shown by the figures.

c) Ask the students if there is any other style of graph that could be used to show the same data. Discuss why the line style is appropriate to show this data and if there is another style that could be equally effective.

Challenge: Make a list of some things that could happen to have a major effect on the trend and the prediction for the world's population over the next 50 years. Explain how these things could cause an increase or a decrease in the population.

Take it forward: Further work using different types of graph can be done with data that shows a more detailed breakdown of population figures for each continent and for selected countries. This will show that there are patterns to the population increase that need to be explained.

People count

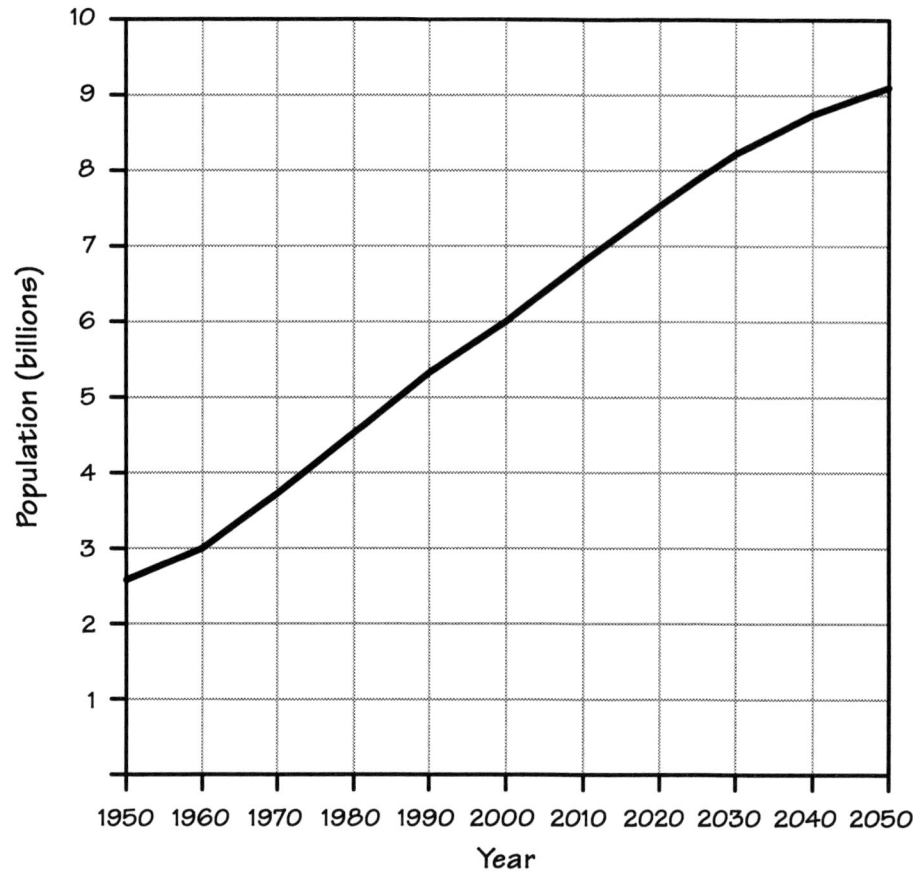

World Population: 1950-2050

Source: U.S. Census Bureau, International Data Base 10-2002.

For each of the years a-f below, mark them on the graph and write down how many people are predicted to be living in the world by each year.

a) The year when you were born.

b) The years when your parents or other older relatives were born.

c) The year when you will leave school at 18 or 19.

d) The year when you will be 30.

e) The year when you will be 65.

f) The year when you will be 80.

The problems with people

Objective:

To understand that world population increase is putting pressure on the Earth's resources and on access to those resources.

What you will need:
Copies of Copymasters 5.4a-b, cut into cards.

Time:
10 minutes

Teaching point:

Ideas about population increase need to be handled with sensitivity, especially in local areas where there have been recent increases. It is important to stress the link between population and resources and how access to additional resources may resolve any problems.

Key words: environment, overpopulation, industrialised, less economically developed, literate

Activity:

a) Begin by asking the students to imagine that there were twice as many of them in the classroom. What differences would that make? Get a list of key words on the board, e.g. lack of space, noise, disagreements, health, movement, etc.

b) Give out the cards from Copymasters 5.4a-b. Explain that they are statements about living conditions in different parts of the world and how the number of people who live in an area can affect the living conditions.

c) The students can rank the cards in the order they think will be most affected by the number of people who live in an area, for example, how the number of people in an area can cause an increase in air pollution. Discuss their ideas.

d) Then get them to rank the list again, this time in the order they think would be the most important to someone of their age who is living in one of the world's least developed countries. Discuss their ideas.

Challenge: Use the titles on the cards to draw a diagram with illustrations, labels and arrows to show how the different problems can be linked, e.g. of air pollution to health.

Take it forward: The students could research their own key facts for other issues such as transport, crime and employment. Further develop ideas about population increase and environmental change by looking at case studies.

Air pollution

Air pollution can give different types of health problems. It is both a local and a global problem and may also be a cause of global warming.

Food

In the world as a whole, one child younger than 5 years old dies from hunger and related causes every 2.7 seconds.

Education

In industrialized countries, 98% of men and 96% of women are able to read and write (they are literate). These figures are down to 60% and 38% in the world's least economically developed countries.

The problems with people

Water

People in 31 countries, making up about 8 percent of the world's population, face severe shortages of freshwater that threaten their health and standard of living. A child born in 2003 has a 1 in 13 chance of being one of them.

Disease

Infectious and parasitic diseases cause 25% of all deaths in the world. There are often no medical services to prevent the diseases or help people to recover from them.

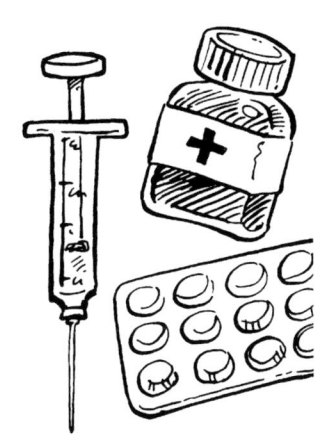

Housing

In many cities in the least economically developed countries, a large percentage of the people live in homes they have built for themselves using scrap materials. The homes are often built in dangerous places, for example, near industry or on steep slopes. They do not have clean water supplies or safe sewerage.

The most, biggest and densest

Objective:

To compare the population totals, size and density in different countries in the world's most populated countries.

What you will need:
Copymaster 5.5 population data pre-loaded onto a spreadsheet.

Time:
10 minutes

Teaching point:

Students can best do this activity by using a spreadsheet with pre-loaded data. If this is not possible, they will need to use a calculator and Copymaster 5.5. If students are not able to access the data themselves, the teacher can lead the activity using an interactive whiteboard.

Key words: population, density, rank, spreadsheet, data

Activity:

a) Provide the students with a data table for the world's top ten most populated countries. Explain that the countries are in rank order of their population.

- Work out the total number of people in these 10 countries. Use the AutoSum tool to do this.

- About what fraction of the world's population live in these ten countries? Discuss if there could be any significance to this.

b) The students can then rank the countries by their area using the Sort tool. They may notice that the list is almost reversed! Discuss the results to see what questions they raise.

c) Explain that because countries are different sizes, it can also be interesting to see which ones have the most people in each square kilometre, i.e. the population density. Demonstrate how to work out density by dividing the population by the area, i.e. Column B/C. Do this for the first country then drag the formula down the column.

- Rank the data again, this time in descending order of population density.

- Discuss the differences with the previous rank orders.

- Think about what questions this raises about the quality of life.

Challenge: Look at atlas maps that show population distribution for one or more of the countries on the list. What extra information do these maps give you about how crowded a country might be?

Take it forward: Work on population density can extend to thinking about differences in rural and urban areas, for example, to compare living in a country where people depend on farming with one in which more people work in industry and services.

Country population data for 2003

All figures have been rounded to make the calculations easier. There are about 6,000,000,000 (6 billion) people in all the countries of the world.

Column A Country	Column B Population total	Column C Area in sq km	Column D Density Column B/C
China	1287000000	9597000	
India	1050000000	3287000	
USA	290000000	9373000	
Indonesia	235000000	1905000	
Brazil	182000000	8512000	
Pakistan	150000000	796000	
Russia	145000000	16996000	
Bangladesh	138000000	144000	
Nigeria	134000000	924000	
Japan	127000000	378000	

Use the figures in the Population Table to do these activities:

a) Work out the total number of people in these 10 countries. If using a spreadsheet, highlight Column B then use the AutoSum tool.

b) About what fraction of the total world's population live in these ten countries? Do you think this could be important?

c) Rank the countries in order of their size. Notice how this compares with the rank order of their populations. What questions do you think that the result raises?

d) Work out the population density in each of these countries. To do this, divide the figures in Column B by the figures in Column C and enter them in column D. Then rank the data in order of population density, the greatest density first. Notice how this compares with the rank orders for population size and area. How might population density be linked to quality of life?

Badger Key Stage 3 Geography Starters

Photos don't lie

Objective:

To explore the information and ideas that can be shown in photos, using ideas about people as a focus.

Teaching point:

Students are constantly presented with images that appear to provide information and ideas. This makes it important that they should be able to take a critical approach to the use of photos and other kinds of visual resources.

What you will need:

Copies of Copymaster 5.6a photo of refugees and 5.6b photo analysis template.

Time:
10 minutes

Key words: source, bias, information, ideas

Activity:

a) Show the students Copymaster 5.6a. Do not tell them anything about it. Give them Copymaster 5.6b, a template. The activity is to think about the photo and complete the template sheet. They can work either individually or in pairs to do this.

b) Discuss the results they have entered on the sheets. Consider:

- How much reliance can be put on the photo as a source of information.

- Reasons for any bias.

- The importance of using a variety of sources when researching information.

c) Tell the students the origin of the photo and the context in which it was taken. It shows a group of Albanian Kosovar refugees in 1999. They were being given identity cards by UNHCR (United Nations High Commission for Refugees) as they made their way home to Albania. The photographer was from the EPA (European Press Agency). Discuss how this information might have been useful when completing the template.

Challenge: Use the template to study other photos, either from text books or websites. The number of photos provided on a particular topic in a text book might raise questions about balance. Find the origin of the photos at the front or back of the book.

Take it forward: This activity can be used as a starting point for developing ideas about migration. Case studies can provide details about why people move and can become refugees.

Photos don't lie

Photos don't lie

Ten questions to ask about a photo

Questions	Tick one of the three answers	Tick
1 Who took the photo?	Works for a business or sells photos	
	Works for a voluntary agency or education	
	A private individual	
2 Where was the photo taken?	I have clear information I trust	
	I can make a guess	
	I have no idea	
3 When was the photo taken	I have clear information about this	
	I can make a guess	
	I have no idea	
4 What motive did they have in taking it?	There is a clear message they want to give	
	There are mixed or confused messages	
	They only want to provide information	
5 How staged is the scene?	The people have been posed for the photo	
	The people are acting completely naturally	
	The scene is completely natural	
6 How typical are the people in the scene?	This is mostly typical for this area	
	This scene is only true for some people	
	The scene is only true for a minority	
7 What did the people think about being photographed?	They were happy to be photographed	
	They did not care	
	They did not want to be photographed	
8 How did the photo make you feel?	It made me very interested in the people	
	It gave me some interest in the people	
	I am not interested at all in the people	
9 How much do you know about the people and place?	I now know much more	
	I know a little more	
	I do not now much more	
10 How much more do you want to know about the people?	I want to know a lot more	
	I want to know some more	
	I don't want to know anything more	

Badger Publishing Limited
26 Wedgwood Way, Pin Green Industrial Estate,
Stevenage, Hertfordshire SG1 4QF
Telephone: 01438 356907
Fax: 01438 747015
www.badger-publishing.co.uk
enquiries@badger-publishing.co.uk

Badger Key Stage 3 Geography Starters - Book 2

ISBN 1 84424 139 4

Text © Fred Martin, Lisa Mitchell, Charlotte Togni and Gary Dawson 2003
Complete work © Badger Publishing Limited 2003

Copyright photos: 1.1 Twelve Apostles, Australia (G. Hellier), 3.3a Johannesburg, South
    Africa (A. Tovy) and 3.3c Mt. Kenya, with giant lobelia in foreground, Kenya, Africa
    (D.C. Poole) © Robert Harding Picture Library; 1.4 Varadero Beach, Matanzas
    Province, Cuba © Donald Nausbaum / Getty Images; 1.5 Sue Earle, Great Cowden
    (J. Giles), 3.3b Homeless in New York (EPA), 3.3d Wiltshire rubbish tip (B.B. Batchelor)
    and 3.6 Albanian Kosovars (EPA) © Press Association Photos; 2.4 Indian earthquake -
    Bhachau, Gugarat (Peter MacDiarmid), 3.5 Shanty Town, Buenos Aires, Argentina
    (Chris Bott) © Rex Features.

Publisher: David Jamieson
Editor: Paul Martin
Designer: Adam Wilmott
Illustrators: Juliet Breese and Adam Wilmott

Printed in the UK.

Badger Starters

For the Key Stage 3 Core Subjects

Badger Maths Starters by Brian Fillis, KS3 Maths Consultant
"Extremely helpful ~ we are recommending them" *KS3 Maths Consultant*

Year 7	ISBN 1 85880 906 1
Year 8	ISBN 1 85880 907 X
Year 9	ISBN 1 85880 908 8

Badger Literacy Starters by Pie Corbett & Sue Dymoke
"Excellent ~ really, really good" *KS3 Literacy Consultant*

Year 7 Word Level	ISBN 1 85880 860 X
Year 7 Sentence Level	ISBN 1 85880 863 4
Year 8 Word Level	ISBN 1 85880 861 8
Year 8 Sentence Level	ISBN 1 85880 864 2
Year 9 Word Level	ISBN 1 85880 862 6
Year 9 Sentence Level	ISBN 1 85880 866 9

Badger Science Starters by John Parker
"I am really impressed and so are a lot of my schools" *KS3 Science Consultant*

Year 7	ISBN 1 85880 353 5
Year 8	ISBN 1 85880 354 3
Year 9	ISBN 1 85880 355 1

For the Key Stage 3 Foundation Subjects

Badger History Starters by Phil Suggitt

Book 1 (with a Y7 focus)	ISBN 1 84424 135 1
Book 2 (with a Y8 focus)	ISBN 1 84424 136 X
Book 3 (with a Y9 focus)	ISBN 1 84424 137 8

Badger Geography Starters
Fred Martin, Lisa Mitchell, Charlotte Togni and Gary Dawson

Book 1 (with a Y7 focus)	ISBN 1 84424 138 6
Book 2 (with a Y8 focus)	ISBN 1 84424 139 4
Book 3 (with a Y9 focus)	ISBN 1 84424 140 8

Badger Religious Education Starters
Helen Morrison, Jo Weir, Karen Saywood & Simone Whitehouse

Teacher Book with Copymasters	ISBN 1 84424 141 6